COWBOYS, COOKSTOVES, & CATASTROPHIES

By Nona Kelley Carver

Designed and produced by Carver Country Poetry.
All poetry and pen and ink illustrations are the
original work of the author. Photo credits beside
each photo, unless taken by the author.

Library of Congress Catalog Card Number: 94-94483
Carver, Nona Kelley, 1936-
Cowboy Poetry • *Cowboys, Cookstoves, & Catastrophies*
Fully illustrated
ISBN 0-9641195-6-0

Published by:
Carver Country Poetry
P.O. Box 115
Mesa, CO 81643-0115

Available at:
The Treasure House
Souvenirs and Gifts
1096 Hwy. 65
Mesa, CO 81643
(970) 268-5642

Printed in Grand Junction, Colorado
by
PrintMasters

With special thanks to Alfred, my loving husband and companion; my family and friends, who will always inspire me to write; to Yule Chaffin, whose unfailing encouragement spurs me on; to the models in my photographs, who wish to remain anonymous; and to Jack and Doris Hart and Linda and Earl Hittle, without whose help, this project would have been impossible.

Nona Kelley Carver

When you step through the open door
That memory leaves ajar,
Please bring your sense of humor
And together we'll go far.

Please set aside a little time
To just sit down, relax.
Disconnect the telephone,
And do turn off the fax.

Return with me to other times,
When life was much more simple.
When we saw joy in smiling eyes,
And noticed every dimple.

About the Author:

Nona Kelley (Grubbs) Carver was born in Colorado. It is still one of her favorite places to be. She learned to read by the light of a kerosene lamp in a cabin built of logs. She, her sister and two brothers rode horses to school. It was at the country school that she met Alfred Carver, who she married in 1953. They have two sons, two daughters-in-law and three grandchildren.

Nona writes from many years of farm and ranch experience. Much of her poetry is drawn from her memories of various people who have crossed her path and enriched her life.

Her entanglements with cows and horses, skunks, goats and hornets have added spice to the verses she refers to as "fiction with a few facts thrown in." Those who know her will recognize the truth.

Her pen and ink cartoon characters are designed to draw the reader more fully into the merriment of the moment.

Cowboys, Cookstoves and Catastrophies is Nona's second book. *The Tarnish On The Golden Years* was published in 1994. It, too, is poetry covering the subjects of Retirement, Wrinkles, and Rotten Memory.

Nona's work has been published in magazines, anthologies and newspapers. The National Library of Poetry requested that she write a poem to include in their new anthology, *Best Poems of 1995*. The Absent Friend was her contribution to this work.

Yule Chaffin
Alaska Press Women, affiliate of
National Federation of Press Women

THE POET AND THE PRINTER

A poet and a printer
Became friends one winter day.
She would write and he would print
The words she had to say.

She would arrive in early morn
With pages written full.
Some of it was serious,
But most of it was "bull."

I'm sure she wore his patience thin.
I couldn't tell the half
Of all the help he was to her,
But he enjoyed a laugh

Each time she brought her nonsense in,
Presented to his press,
More challenges, more work to do,
While he was under stress.

Her great appreciation
Is only told in part.
Her gratitude is thus expressed
To Printer, Friend, Jack Hart.

Glen and Elnora Carver on their 50th
Wedding Anniversary.

DEDICATION

Dedicated to Glen and Elnora Carver, who owned and operated a ranch and dairy farm in western Colorado for nearly fifty years.

CONTENTS

ENDORSEMENTS

Now some folks have endorsements.
Believe me, I have none.
A writer finds those hard to get
Until the work is done.

My friends and my relation,
They always like my stuff,
'Tho some of them do realize
That much of it is "guff."

They giggle and they guffaw
And read between the lines.
They hope my sense of humor
Won't get me any fines!

They're tolerant and helpful
For they have been there, too.
But if you read my poetry,
The rest is up to you!

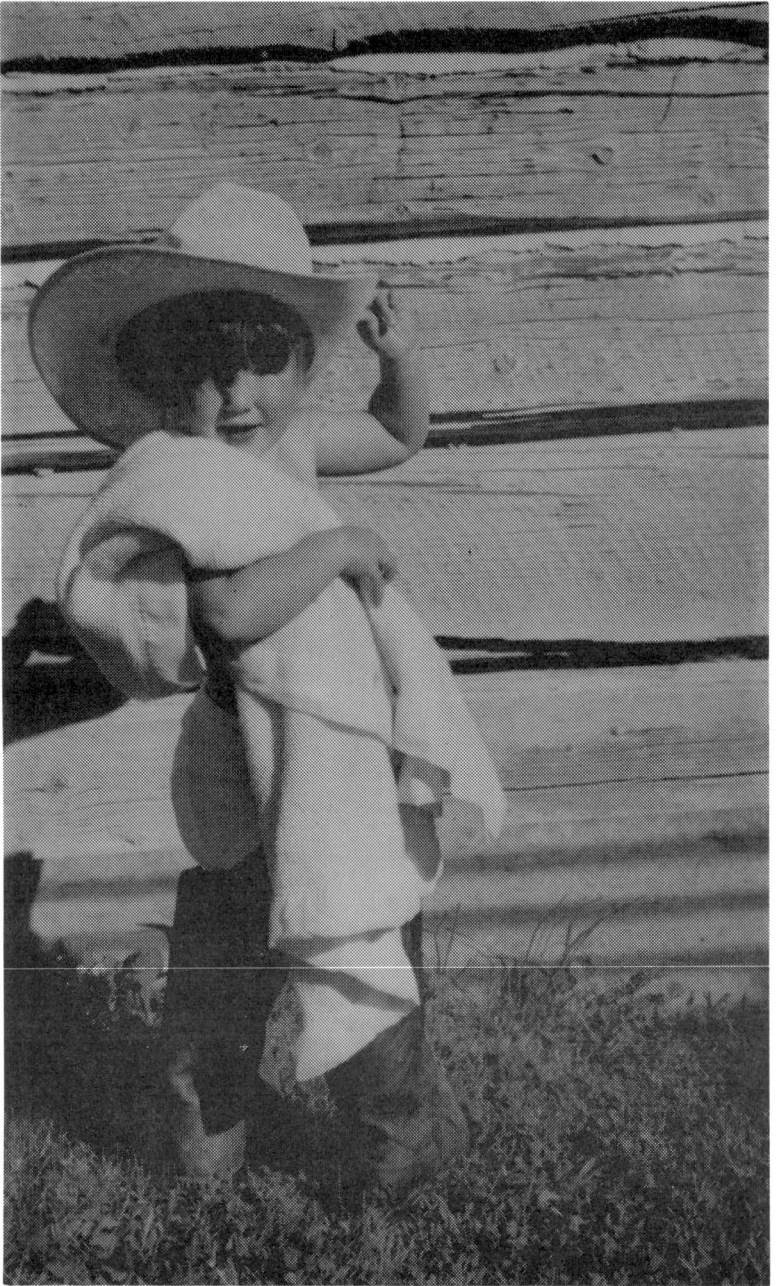

FOREWORD

Oh, to be a Cowboy!
Each little person knows
It looks like fun just to be one,
And so the notion grows.

Somewhere between the diaper,
And entry in first grade,
They may want boots and holsters,
They see as tools of trade.

Some do outgrow the notion.
To them, my sympathy!
But those who love the open sky
Will choose this destiny.

The author, ready to help bring cattle in.

COWBOY POET

You ask how I got started?
It seemed like fun to me,
To just describe on paper,
The open sky, all free.

How I became a poet?
I swear I don't know how.
I just picked up the pencil,
And started thinkin' cow.

Those years of haulin' yearlin's
And broke-down stuff to town
Just flowed down through the pencil
And turned the paper brown.

I didn't study grammar,
For sure, that's plain to see.
I just work out the rhythm,
Put thoughts down as they be.

I'm not that great accomplished,
As plain as an old shoe.
I just like to come and tell
Of things I see as true.

A ranchin' life is mighty hard,
But pleasure full, you see.
You can't waste time with worryin',
Just let your soul run free.

There's work from early mornin'
That lasts until twilight.
But ranchers never will give in.
They put up quite a fight!

They tend the land and cattle,
Then return home to sup.
In tomorrow's early daylight,
They'll see the sun come up.

They put their kids on horseback,
Before the age of four.
They help the lonely stranger,
Who may come to their door.

The grandpas and the grandmas,
Have done their share, no doubt.
But come the day for herdin',
They'll help put cattle out.

Some days the words keep flowin'
From early until late.
Sometimes there are none at all.
Something has closed the gate!

When I think I have it,
I jot it down real slick.
For my poor mind won't hold it,
The memory's gone too quick.

At break of day, I labor.
I try to do my best.
Sometimes can't shut off at night
To get a little rest!

Then there's the fear of editors
Who alter all your lines
And leave your poem like a fork
With several missing tines.

A poet's life is easy,
Compared to punchin' cows.
But please, let's not get technical
With all the whys and hows!

OLE' BUFORD

Ole' Buford was a trusty hound
Who could hold wolves at bay.
He stood sweating in the dog yard
On a sweltering summer day.

Miz Beulah was his mistress.
She liked to dress up big.
She'd bathed and rouged and powdered,
And donned her favorite wig.

She'd polished nails, applied perfume,
Put on her newest gown.
For she was out to have some tea
With fancy folks up town!

She had just headed for the door,
Then recalled in despair,
She'd promised Sam before he left,
She'd water Buford, there.

She filled a bucket to the brim,
And fearing she'd be late,
She tiptoed to the dog yard,
And opened up the gate.

Now Buford's pan had gone bone dry,
And Beulah made no sense
Of why he'd rolled it here and there
Back by the corner fence.

Watching the hound, she stepped in
And didn't see the hole,
Went sprawling face down on the ground,
And then began to roll.

Now Buford liked his dog yard,
Where he could play and dig,
But he got all excited
When Beulah lost her wig!

He grabbed it, threw it in the air,
Caught it, began to chomp.
He tossed it in his potty place,
And then began to stomp.

He dropped it in the water
She'd spilled when she fell down,
And Beulah knew that nevermore
She'd wear that wig to town.

For Buford thought it was alive!
He'd done his best to kill it!
Protecting Beulah was his task,
And he'd tried hard to fill it!"!

SHARING

Mama says we need to share
As we start up life's path.
Sister and I do try hard,
Even in our bath.

She really doesn't take much room,
She's such a little thing.
And out here we don't worry much
About a "bathtub ring."

Mom drew the water from the well
And warmed it up just right.
We must be sure to tell her thanks,
And give her hugs tonight.

Our daddy will want kisses
When he returns to camp.
Our mom will brush and curl
Our hair, while it is feeling damp.

Here comes mama with a towel.
I'm sure she'll help us dry.
And if we have to share that, too,
We'll give it our best try!

THE BOOTS

These boots were worn by both our boys,
As each one grew in turn.
They're fairly worn, and 'way too small,
But I could never burn

Them up or toss them out,
For they hold memories dear,
Of little boys we loved and held,
As they grew more each year.

The boys fulfilled our fondest dreams.
Brought sunshine to our life.
And we knew then, they would grow up,
And someday take a wife.

They fed the calves and spread the hay,
Hauled water to the barn.
They did their chores and liked to hear
Their grandpa spin a yarn.

They would come in all tired and hot,
But hope lit up their eyes
When they would smell some home made bread,
Or spot some apple pies.

They worked and helped us, did their share.
They did not sulk or pout.
As long as there is light and air,
Their boots, I'll not throw out!

THE OLE' NEVADA COWBOY

He said he was a cowboy,
Though he'd been known to jest.
We reckoned he'd known hosses,
Both orneriest and best.

His boots and jeans were dusty,
His shirt was slick with grime.
If he knew how to launder,
He didn't have the time!

As he sat sippin' coffee,
His beard was in a braid;
Rawhide thongs held up his jeans,
Surprisingly, they stayed!

He didn't care for bosses,
A few had got him riled.
He spent his time with hosses,
The gentle and the wild.

We mounted up and rode away,
For home was many a mile
From the ole' Nevada cowboy,
With his coffee and his smile.

© 1993 Nona Kelley Carver

THE POTBELLIED STOVE

Many a bunkhouse and cabin
From Memphis to Mexican Cove,
Have been warmed by a fire in the evening,
Built up in a potbellied stove.

Many a man at the woodpile,
Has worked off his anger and wrath.
And many a boy has been branded,
Just as he stepped out of his bath!

Many a shirt has dried by it.
Without it home wasn't much.
It served as a handy disposal,
For papers and clutter and such.

On mornings the ground was all covered
With inches of new-fallen snow,
We carefully put in the tender
And fanned to make sure it would go.

We polished it, took out the ashes,
Then stood back to just catch our breath,
For the potbellied stove in our cabin's
What kept us from freezin' to death!

THE HORSE TRAILER

If a cowboy's all cooped up,
His boss seems like a jailer.
He's likely to pack up and move,
In his trusty old horse trailer.

His trailer' s used for many things
Besides just hauling horses.
It might be used to shelter him
From weather's wicked forces.

They come in great variety,
From nice to rolling rust.
Depends if owner's big time rich,
Or gone completely bust.

It may have hauled an old mare home,
When she had lost her poop.
It may get parked in the back yard,
Be used as chicken coop!

It may move furniture and stoves,
Perhaps a broke-down tractor.
But it is just a tool of trade,
The cowboy is the actor.

And we all know there'll come a time
When he'll need a replacement.
But he may keep the rusty frame
To haul junk from the basement.

© 1994 NKC
Home Barber Shop

18

HOME BARBER SHOP

When I began to cut his hair,
It was black as the night.
I thought him truly handsome,
A trim and dashing sight.

I told him that I wasn't trained
In ways of cutting hair.
But he worked as a cowboy then,
And said, "The cows won't care."

So I began the trimming.
Dark hair piled on the floor.
He said, "That's fine. Just cut it,"
I shaped it up some more.

He didn't make appointments,
I cut when we had time.
I liked to see him neat and trim,
And didn't charge a dime.

Many years have come and gone,
And hair once black as night
Gave way to little wisps of gray,
Then turned to silver white.

He's still as handsome as before,
This gentleman, my friend.
He's been my life companion,
And will be 'til the end.

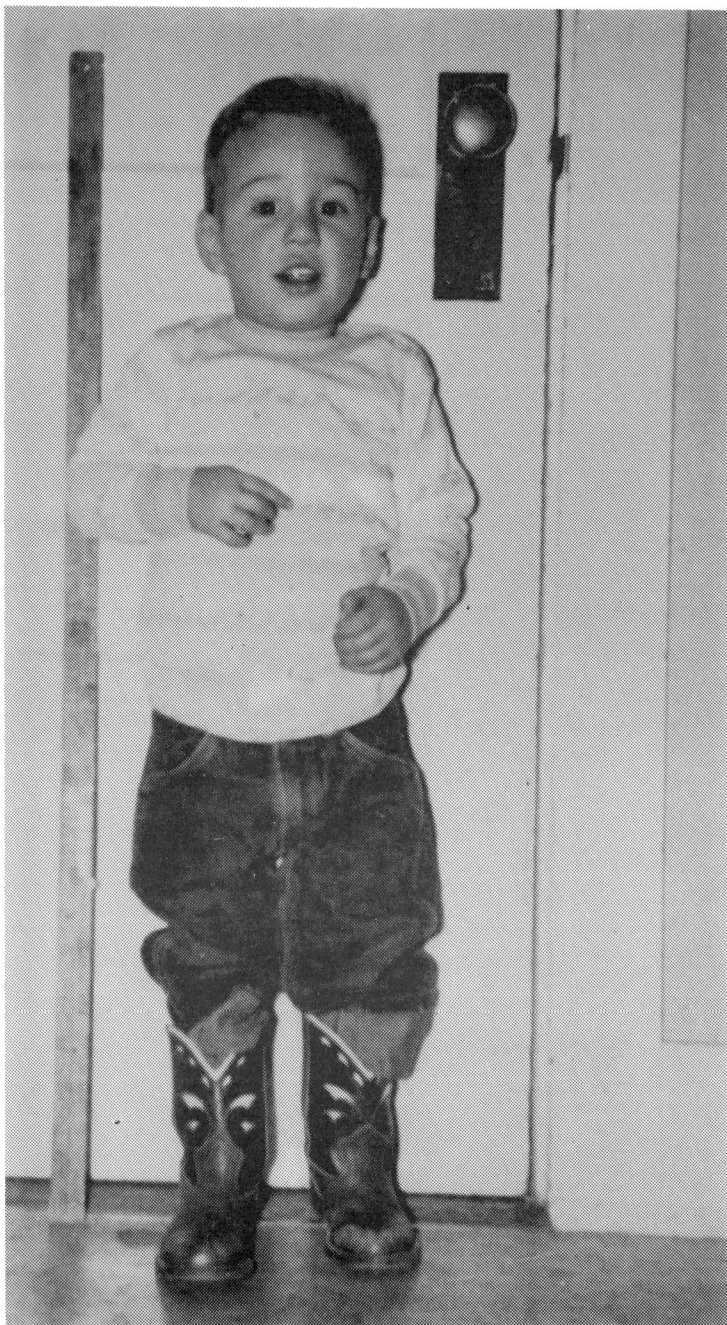

STRETCHIN' UP

I'm stretchin' up so I can be
A man just like my dad.
I want to do some things I can't
While such a little lad.

I want to climb up on a horse
And bring the cattle in.
Dad says I'll soon be big enough,
But I just don't know when!

And "one day" seems forever
When you are very small.
I want to grow up right away
And be all straight and tall.

Mom says it happens fast enough.
A boy becomes a man.
But I still want to rush it some,
And hurry if I can.

For I can't wait to ride along
And try to do my part.
A year or two seems awful long.
It's NOW I want to start!

©1994 N.K.C.
perpetual Motion

PERPETUAL MOTION

He must have hit the floor running,
On a cold and frosty morn.
I doubt the Doc could catch him
On the day that he was born!

He had no time to dawdle,
Unless going toward the school.
But he didn't mind the recess,
Or break the Golden Rule.

And when the day was over,
He rushed so he could play.
For he knew pleasant pastimes
Beat school work any day!

He never shirked a duty.
At work, he was a whiz.
If you saw tracks dragging slow,
You knew they were not his.

He hurried in the morning
When he reached to get his hat.
Spit never reached the sidewalk,
It dried up as he spat.

Rushing to the river,
Or down the railroad tracks,
You scarcely could catch sight of him.
He could not pause, relax.

He did have time for fishing,
A high priority.
He had the time for wishing
They'd grab his hook, you see.

He only slept a little,
Some said he didn't try.
On nights the moon was really full,
He just eyeballed the sky.

He was always in a hurry
Everywhere he went.
He rode, "Hell-bent-for-leather,"
Like he was demon sent!

When they nail the lid on his coffin,
He'll look them in the eye,
And they will hear an awesome voice
Call down from the sky,

"Can't you hurry with that hammer?
What makes you work so slow?
Let's see some more wrist action
In that scene far down below!"

SECRETS

You want to know a secret?
I heard our daddy say
That it is almost Christmas!
At least, it's on the way.

I know we must be very good.
Remember not to pout.
I'd hate to have them buy a doll
And have to throw it out!

I heard there'll be a Christmas tree
With candles for a light,
And stories of a shining star
From that first Christmas night.

We'll draw a picture for Grandpa,
And one for Mom and Dad.
I wish that Grandma were here, too,
So Mom would not feel sad.

We'll hang our stockings up at night
Before we go to bed.
Remember it's a secret, now,
So don't tell what I've said.

THE AUCTIONEER

An auctioneer with store-bought teeth
Arrived late for a sale.
The crowd sat there expecting him
Quite soon to start his wail.

The buyers had come early.
They had looked at the stock.
Checked out the vaccinations,
Examined hoof and hock.

The barn crew in bifocals,
Were set to catch each bid.
The clerk had settled in nearby.
Behind a desk, she hid.

The auctioneer had just begun,
But noticed something wrong!
His teeth were buckin' like a colt
And messin' up his song!

They rose and hesitated,
And then those ornery teeth
Began to circle 'round his tongue
Just like a Christmas wreath!

He paused and gained control again.
His nose began to itch.
The biddin' started heatin' up
And reached a fever pitch

When those teeth just deserted him.
They flew right past his mouth!
The auctioneer was lookin' north
His teeth were headed south!

They bit the clerk on their way down,
Creating some dissention,
And started for the gaping crowd
And places we wont mention!

The saleyard dog caught up with them
Just as they reached the dirt,
But lost them as a man up front
Lassoed them with his shirt.

They rinsed them in some lemonade
And hung them on a rack.
And when they dried, again he tried,
'Tho some had turned their back.

The auctioneer resumed his cry,
Decided on next trip
He'd bring along a king-size tube
Of super denture-grip!

©1995 Nona Kelley Carver

©1994 NKC
Branding Time

BRANDING TIME

Some cowboys truly dread the day
When calves they have to brand.
Some half-grown steers can drag you
Quite near The Promised Land!

Can't you see and taste the thistles?
On your teeth feel the sand?
When once you rope that dogie
And attach it to a brand?

The bawlin' of the mamas,
The smell of burning hide?
Just think of all the truama
Some folks would feel inside!

But brandin's a necessity,
Not as to "if" or "whether,"
But choose your day most carefully.
It's worse in ugly weather.

And once the irons are heated,
The poor calf on his side,
Some folks just can't stay seated.
They want to run and hide!

But once the task is over,
They'll know they've done their best.
For brandin' is a fact of life,
When you live 'way out West!

© 1994 Nona Kelley Carver

©1994 NKC
cowboy Joe

COWBOY JOE

His horse was just the fastest,
Really built for speed.
He galloped fast amd cantered slow,
A great and trusty steed.

His hat, it was the biggest,
The blackest and the best.
No wonder some folks thought of him
As "Giant of the West."

Some folks thought that he was mean,
And drank from witches' brew.
Truth was, he wouldn't harm a flea,
Or speak unkind to you.

His heart was just as gentle
As a precious newborn lamb.
He'd never seek to hurt or press
You in an unkind scam.

He worked from early morning
Until the dark of night.
Took pleasure in just helping folks
Caught in some toilsome plight.

He's gone now, down that lonesome road,
But I can hear him yet,
Singing in my memory
Sweet songs I'll not forget.

JONAH

Jonah was a hound dog
He measured six feet long.
And when he bayed, it was relayed
As Jonah's hound dog song.

He liked to have you scratch his back.
He'd nuzzle with his nose.
Sometimes he'd growl and snarl a bit
To keep you on your toes.

He wasn't much for salesmen,
Who might come sneakin' round.
They packed their bags and traveled quick,
When threatened by this hound!

Then Jonah would just drop his head,
And with expression grim,
Stand laughing on the inside,
That folks were scared of him.

His owner was a cowboy,
Who liked to rope and ride.
He was content when Jonah went
And trotted by his side.

Now Jonah disliked rattlers,
He and Charlie knew
Whenever he encountered one,
You'd find it in your stew!

©1994NKC
Jonah II

For Charlie, at the cook shack
Was often short of grub.
He got tired of plain old beans
That bubbled in his tub!

So he and Jonah hunted.
They found all sorts of things
To stock up the old larder,
And grease the wagon springs.

They rendered lard from ground hogs,
That boiled with their beans,
And fed all that were hungry,
Who questioned not their means.

You never knew at mealtime,
When you sat down to dine
If you were having sage hen,
Or maybe porcupine...

He called it "beef extender,"
Or "rabbit's foot tofu."
But Charlie and the hound dog
Were the only ones that knew.

They topped themselves at Christmas.
Roast pheasant, nuts of pine.
And it was wild when Jonah smiled,
And kinfolks came to dine!

RAIN

Lord, you know we need some rain
On cropland now and then.
The Good Book says that it will fall,
But doesn't tell us when.

The cows are almost out of grass.
The well is going dry.
And one more month just like we've had
Will make me want to cry.

I think I see a little cloud
And hope begins to rise,
But lookin' closer, see it's dust
That shrouds the evenin' skies.

Mom says her beans are dryin' up.
She's lookin' so forlorn.
She's noticed leaves are rollin' too,
On spindly stalks of corn.

We hear they're gettin' rain back East,
With rivers runnin' full.
You sure I heard it right, now, Lord,
That it's not "cock and bull?"

We'll need a lot of calves next year,
Our losses to regain.
And Lord, we know it's up to you,
But please send us some rain!

MAMA'S BOOTS

When will I be big enough
To wear my mama's boots?
And drive my daddy's pick-up
And blow the horn that toots?

I wish that it were yesterday
And I was not so small.
Why is it that I have to wait
To grow up strong and tall?

I've heard there is a cradle
And new brother on the way.
I'll let him ride my rockin' horse
So he will want to stay.

We'll take him to the Rodeo
To watch my daddy ride.
We'll play outside with puppies
And find where kittens hide.

I know my mom will help me.
And maybe when I'm grown,
She'll let me drive on into town
And buy boots of my own!

©1994 NKC
Gardner

PARDNER

He talked a lot of Pardner,
Though none had ever seen
Him walking with another soul,
The many miles between.

His cabin and the main corral,
Or to fences he must mend.
They wondered if the tales were true,
Or was he "spouting wind?"

He touted Pardner's merits,
On each new detail dwelled.
They knew for sure no woman
Could stand the way he smelled!

He told them Pardner was the best,
To keep him warm at night.
And if defend his home he must,
Old Pardner'd help him fight!

He reckoned Pardner'd surely have
A halo up above.
Yes, Pardner really seemed to be
His one and only love.

It wasn't 'til the old man died
And they removed his coat,
That papers from his pocket told
That Pardner was his goat!

©1994 NKC
The old Campfire

THE OLD COWPOKE

The old cowpoke sat dreaming
Of busy days gone by.
His fragile frame had bent with time,
But there was twinkle in his eye.

He used to court a dimpled lass,
A truly lovely girl.
Thoughts of her still thrilled his heart
And kept his thoughts awhirl.

She had been a mere sixteen
When he was twenty-four.
He stole first kisses at a dance
Held on the school house floor.

He'd asked to meet her ma and pa,
He'd asked them for her hand.
But they preferred an older man,
A rancher who had land.

He'd tipped his hat and rode away,
Then hastened to recall,
He'd seen a tear form in her eye,
And on her bodice fall.

He must convince her parents
He was worthy of her hand.
Each day, he worked his hardest.
Each night, he dreamed and planned.

©1994 NKC
The Old Couple II

He asked her in a letter
If she would care to wait
Until her folks accepted him,
And set a wedding date.

Her answer made him walk on air,
And drove fear from his mind.
Her pa, she said, had chanced to see
The rancher was unkind.

They'd have his blessing, now, she said,
Throughout a happy life.
He'd lost no time to ride out there
And claim her for his wife.

Together, they had spent their time,
Until that sad, long day
When angels same to call for her,
And took her far away.

He misses her, but of his life,
She still remains a part.
In memory, he sees her yet.
He holds her in his heart.

ROCKING CHAIR RHAPSODIES

The old cowboy and his guitar
Had traveled many years.
The songs he'd struggled to perform
Had brought some smiles and tears.

His checkered shirt was faded,
His jeans were near threadbare.
And you could see hide peekin' through
A small hole here and there.

He'd carried all his music
Right up there in his head.
But sometimes now, he can't recall
The words, or what they said.

He still sings and stomps a bit,
And hums a little tune.
But mostly, now, he sits and waits
For lunch to come at noon.

He was quite a dandy,
When he was in his prime.
Pretty gals, he'd courted,
He'd showed them a good time.

They'd flocked around and followed
Him where 'ere he went.
They'd vied for his attention,
And loving letters sent.

But one by one, they'd married
Some fellow down the street.
Chose somewhat more stable men,
Who had less itchy feet.

It's hard to raise a family
While goin' on the road.
So he just traveled on alone,
His guitar was his load.

He'd sung in all the night spots,
Ft. Worth to Tennessee.
Never hit the big time,
Just was not meant to be.

He'd tried his hand at writin'
A new song to be sung.
A song to thrill the entire world.
His bell had never rung.

He's seen a lot of scenery
Along the railroad track,
Always, he was goin',
Or thumbin' his way back.

He still strums and mumbles,
This lonesome, would be, star,
Just restin' in his rocker,
With his battered old guitar.

THE FARM

As a couple still quite young,
We bought a little farm.
Our sons were small, and we tried hard,
To keep them safe from harm.

The farm house sat there needing paint,
'Though part of it was logs.
The sunshine warmed the back side up,
And beds of cats and dogs.

We had a little dairy there,
A herd of Holstein cows.
Back in those days, we learned real quick
To work when time allows!

Mama planted gardens,
And Daddy tilled the soil.
The children helped us with the chores.
Together, we would toil.

Rusty was our cowdog.
He did the best he could.
Dogs well trained can help you more,
At times, than hired man would.

Looking back may bring a tear,
But no cause for alarm.
Some happy days we spent back then,
Together on the farm.

MY FEELINGS

Feelings, unpredictable,
Color up the way
I look at you, you look at me,
As we go through the day.

Sometimes my world is upside down,
And enemies are there
Behind the bookshelf or the wall,
Perhaps beneath the stair.

They lurk under the covers
When I climb into bed,
And thoughts of being naughty
Just slip into my head!

Depression, such an ugly thing,
Creeps in to steal my joy.
Do you think when I grow up,
I'll wish I were a boy?

I don't think so. What is the cause
For all this consternation?
When they were passing feelings out,
I got one called "frustration!"

©1994 N.K.S.
Internal Revenue Service

I brought form # 00069007-01 so you can
verify your losses for the I.R.S.

INTERNAL REVENUE SERVICE

Someone somewhere back in time
Created Income Tax.
It makes us work from dawn to dusk
Unable to relax.

It pays for all the Congressmen
Who think up many ways
To use our funds and vote themselves
Meanwhile, another raise!

We work and save and try to build
Ourselves a big nest egg.
But Uncle dips his hand right in
And knocks us down a peg.

We try again to raise our voice
And vote the padding out,
But find our efforts are in vain.
We need a lot more clout!

We do not have the answer yet,
And tend to feel quite nervous
Each time a letter arrives from
Internal Revenue Service!

©1995 Nona Kelley Carver

©1995 N.K.C.
Rusty

RUSTY

Rusty was our cow-dog.
He liked to run and play
As soon as all the work was done
On any given day.

His favorite game was "Fling-it."
He didn't make a sound
When he jumped up to catch it,
It seldom touched the ground.

Another game he liked as well,
Is known as "hide and seek."
The boys would send him
'round the house,
So he could never peek.

They would hide and he would search,
Until he sought them out.
It never seemed to take him long.
He traced their scent, no doubt!

Whenever an old rogue got out,
It mattered not, I guess,
If I was wearin' blue jeans,
Or even my best dress.

For Rusty did the runnin'.
He knew each quick command.
I just stood there smilin'.
I needn't turn a hand.

© 1994 N.K.C.
Rusty II

For he knew all the critters,
And just where they should be.
I'd just open up the gate.
He'd take them in, you see.

He helped us when we sorted calves.
He nipped the lagging steers.
Most certainly, he earned his keep,
And helped us through the years.

He went to bring in milk cows,
And worked real careful, slow.
He knew their dispositions,
And where each one should go.

He knew all our vehicles,
From the truck down to the jeep.
And when they started up our drive,
He didn't make a peep.

But let a stranger dare approach,
He barked a sharp alarm.
He felt he was protecting us
From any unknown harm.

It was a sad and lonely day,
When Rusty had to go.
But that's the way it is with folks,
And dogs down here below.

But if dogs have a heaven,
I know just where he'll be...
Restin' in the cooling shade
Of a lovely willow tree.

The Hornet Nest
© 1994 N.K.C.

THE HORNET NEST

The hornets gathered on a stump
To have a little chat.
They drank a bit of apple juice
They'd stolen from the cat.

The queen said to the workers,
"We'll need to build a nest.
The place beneath the outhouse bench
Just looks to me the best."

So they began their project,
As all good hornets do.
They worked with care, day after day,
Admired it as it grew.

The people seemed quite nervous,
When they would make their call.
But each one made their visit,
From the biggest to the small.

The queen had warned them not to sting,
'Though they were very tempted.
It seemed like such a little thing,
But her wishes, theirs, pre-empted.

Now Harry Hornet liked to flit
Through flowers, as he flew.
Became somewhat a nuisance,
The bigger that he grew!

The Hornet Nest II
© 1994 N.K.C.

64

He disliked all the orders.
They simply weren't his style!
He wanted to investigate
Each thing within a mile.

He flirted with the females.
They nixed his swift advance.
They bade him to come later,
When he had learned to dance.

He tantalized the mailman,
And found old Pedro's still.
He crawled along among the hops,
And quickly drank his fill.

He couldn't fly a straight line
When he returned that night,
But did get home and slip in bed
Before it got daylight.

One day when the cook came out
To get some sweet relief,
He stung her on the bottom!
She screamed beyond belief!

And later in the evenin',
When men had gone to town,
She lit the match that cooked his goose,
And burned the outhouse down!

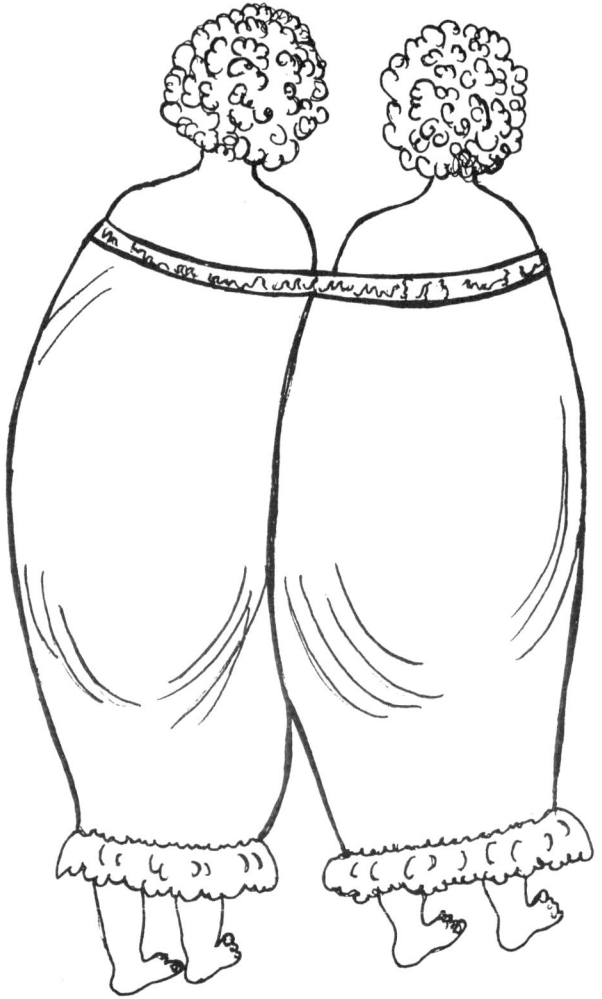

©1994 NKC
Grandma's
Bloomers

GRANDMA'S BLOOMERS

Bloomers were a big affair,
For she was fairly wide.
She cut and sewed and stretched the cloth
As she wriggled down inside.

They were not fancy, as you see,
Just made of flour sack.
But they were snug and quite draft free,
Just clothing on her back.

She wore them to the chicken house,
When she went for the eggs.
Then checked to see when she returned,
No ticks had climbed her legs.

Now Grandma didn't stomp or dance,
It was against her rule.
She cooked and swept and did her part,
Then sent us off to school.

But she could get some chuckles in.
We loved to hear her laugh!
We thought her jokes the funniest,
And cried while bent in half!

© 1994 NKC
Grandma's
Bloomers II

She baked good bread and tasty pies,
Stored in a cupboard, there.
She made us wash and clean our nails,
And braided up our hair.

She let us try her bloomers on
So we could have some fun,
And wore her next-best, well worn drawers
To make her outhouse run.

She had a pair with baggy legs
That came below her knees.
She wore those on the cool, fall days,
When there might be a breeze.

For Grandma was quite proper,
When she strolled into town,
Until the day elastic broke,
And drawers came tumbling down!

She just stepped out and snatched them up
And put them in her purse.
We laughed so hard, she thought she might
Just have to call the hearse!

'Though many years have passed since then,
We still recall the day.
For Grandma's face turned cherry red,
As she went on her way!

© 1994 N.K.C.
The Skunk

THE SKUNK

Our son once drove our car to school
So he could come home early.
The scent he smelled as he drove home
Made him feel downright squirrelly!

I joined him and we went to town,
So he could test for college.
How the car could smell so bad
Was just beyond our knowledge!

We went to where he took his test.
The Prof. turned up his nose.
It seemed the scent had followed us
As odor in our clothes!

I drove up to the beauty shop,
To keep a short appointment.
Some gal remarked as I walked by,
"She must use skunk oil ointment."

Once I had backtracked to the car,
I rolled the window down.
Then found a note that said in part,
"Get this car out of town!"

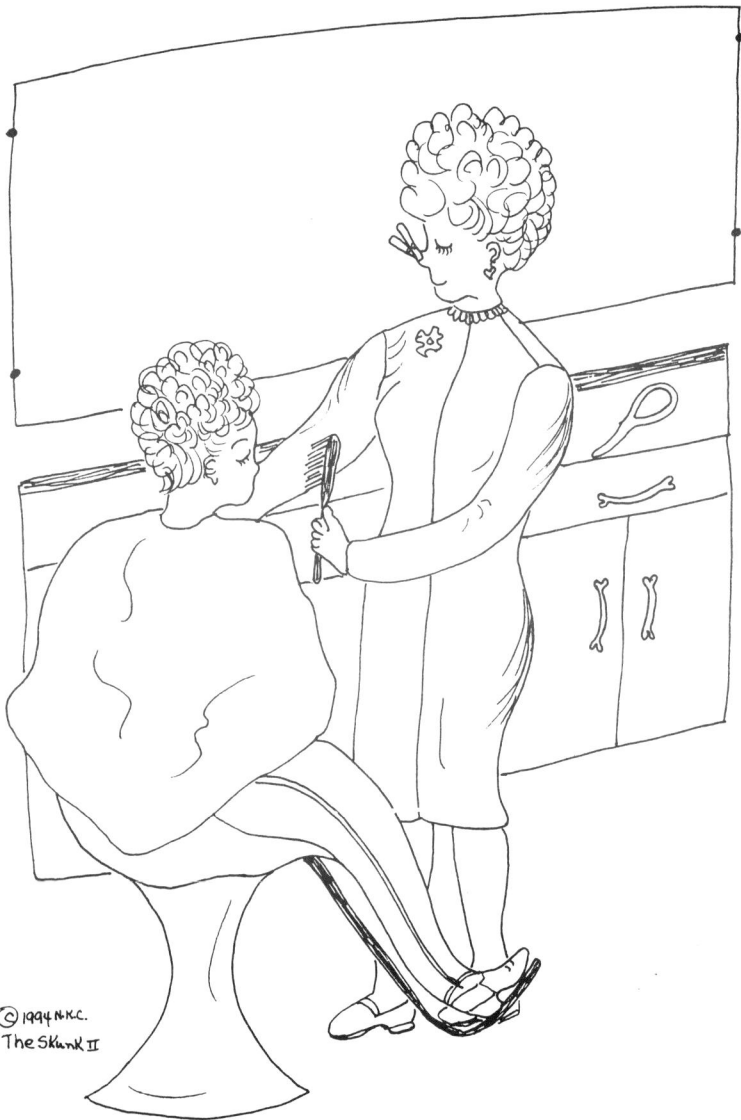

© 1994 N.K.C.
The Skunk II

These scenes repeated of themselves.
They lasted days and days.
We tried to get the odor out,
Who knows how many ways!

Finally, our son returned
To school, where he was told
A prankster had laid out a skunk
On our car's manifold.

One quick peek beneath the hood,
A shovel for remains,
We scraped the skunk right out of there,
Hosed down the ugly stains.

Someday, the prankster will get his.
I'm certain that he will.
I hope the odor's as intense,
And just as hard to kill!

MUD PIES

Mama caught us by the barn
Just makin' some mud pies.
So now we've had to take a bath.
I got soap in my eyes.

Of course, we were just playin',
Not even thinkin' none
About how she would clean us up,
Or get the washin' done.

We didn't think of "messy,"
Or need for cleaner duds.
And we're too short for washboards,
And washtubs full of suds.

I guess she has her reasons
For foulin' up our play.
So we will think of other things
To do this rainy day.

I hope she will forgive us.
I'd miss her special lovin'.
Oh boy! It seems to me I smell
Some cookies in the oven!

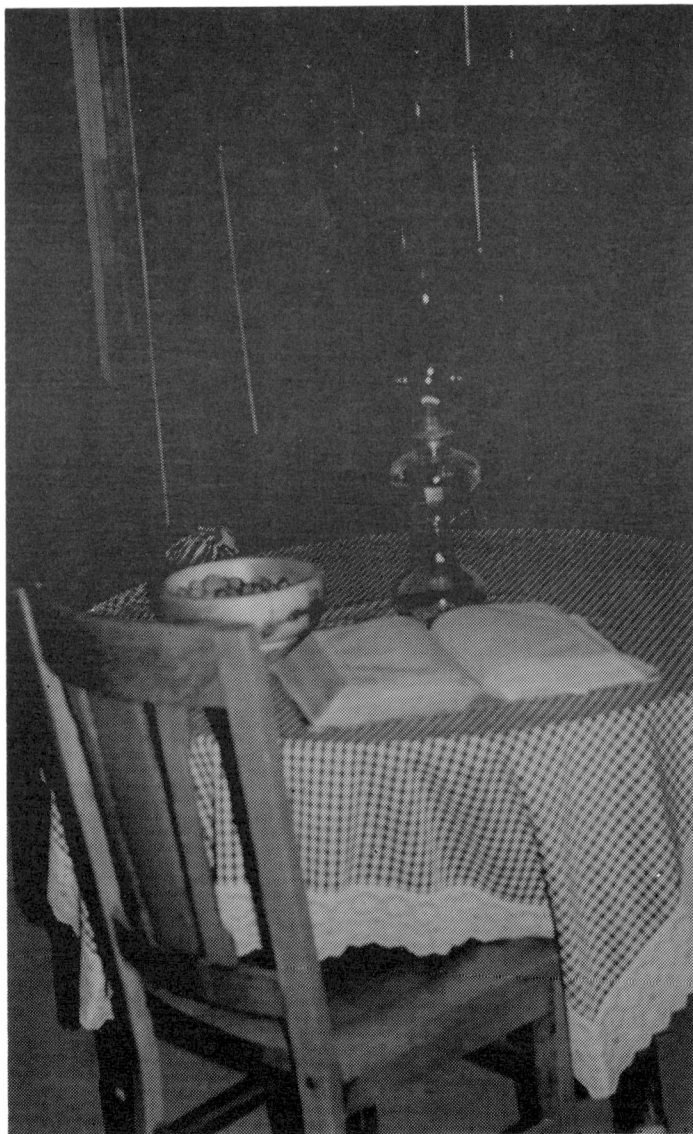

THE FAMILY BIBLE

Great-Great-Grandfather Townsend Hall,
When young and small our nation,
Purchased a Bible to pass down
To each new generation.

It was to pass to eldest son,
In each new family.
The principles he asked be taught
Were faith, hope, charity.

He almost lost the Bible once,
This book from our Life-Giver.
It went down in a wagon bed
In the Mississippi River!

He fished it out and dried it.
None of it's pages lost.
It's principles impressed the man
More than the price it cost.

It came down as he wanted.
To Matthew, Hoyt, and Glen.
Alfred and I have it now,
It's message held within.

Someday, we too, will pass it on.
May it's message never cease.
May those who read it know the joy
Of everlasting peace.

© 1994 N.K.C.
The Red Milk Cow

THE RED MILK COW

The old red cow was ornery.
Each time she got the chance,
When I sat down to milk her,
She did her "kick and dance"

Routine that always spilled the milk.
Then she would swing and swat
Me with her super nasty tail,
Her price for milk I got!

When I approached to bring her in,
She'd get a mean-eyed look.
And she had names, but they're not fit
To print in any book!

She looked at stanchions like a bull
Looks at a maverick calf.
If I talked now 'til Doomsday,
I couldn't tell the half!

Once, when I was milkin',
She kicked me so high,
She left her ugly footprint
Right up there on my thigh.

She had a way about her
That baffled me each morn
Until I took a trusty stick
And whacked her on the horn!

I'd gather up the milk stool,
Then show I had the stick.
She knew what it was good for.
She learned that pretty quick!
  Once, I just forgot it,
And did she lay me low!
She rolled me in the cow pies,
With swift and mighty blow!
  She had no use for fences,
And durn her ornery hide,
She thought grass was the greenest,
Right on the other side.
  She'd push and stretch and wallow
Until she made it through.
With eyes all glassy, hollow,
She'd turn and look at you.
  Each year when her calf was born,
She would be meaner yet.
She'd paw and stomp
and shake her head.
Her baby, you'd not pet!
  I started celebratin'
The day my husband said,
"Let's send her to the sale yard."
Farewell, to mean Old Red!
  Sometimes, it seems, I see her yet.
I grin when I think of her.
Visualizing that old cow
Ground into lean hamburger!

Mom
©1995 N.K.S.

MOM

Sometimes life gets tedious
When calves and critters die.
Mom offers up some solace,
With home made apple pie.

She may have canned tomatoes
Or helped haul in the hay,
But still puts out the effort,
It seems that's just her way.

She sees how her folks struggle,
From the biggest to the small.
She wants to help each special one.
To her, they all stand tall.

She rises early mornin's,
And milks the family cow.
It gives her time for prayin'
They'll save the ranch somehow.

For she, too, feels the burden,
The awful load of debt.
But thinks that maybe someday,
The ranch will pay off yet.

She'd helped to brand the cattle,
Some earlier this spring.
She'd filled the vaccine needles,
Did every sort of thing.

She figures out the taxes,
And how we're gonna pay,
And hopes we have the money
When April comes our way!

She patches up the blue jeans,
And mends our tattered shirts.
I never see her cryin'
But I know, inside, she hurts.

Though life is hard, no whinin'
Slips out between her lips.
She just keeps on tryin'
And makes those weekly trips

Down to get necessities,
That needed stuff from town,
Like flour, sugar, pork and beans,
Then bakes our biscuits brown.

She has a little garden,
And hoes each weedy spot.
Matters not if windy,
Or the day is super hot.

If cookin' up some dumplin's
Or maybe bakin' spuds,
She wears her checkered apron.
For her, no fancy duds!

For special things like cookies,
Or maybe homemade bread,
We truly try to thank her.
Enough cannot be said!

She helps us with our homework,
By day or dim lamp light.
Better never sass her,
She'll set you straight, alright!

She'll feed you when you're hungry,
And lift you when you're down.
She'll help you with the plowin'
That turns the fields to brown.

She'll hang in there for harvest,
And work from sun to sun.
Keep pitchin', stretchin', tryin',
Until the job is done.

Oh, how much we'd miss her,
If she should go away.
But she'll hold out 'til angels come
And take her home to stay.

SISTERS

You're feeling sad. I'm sorry.
Sometimes I feel sad, too.
Mom says we should think happy thoughts
When we are feeling blue.

Let's think about the pony
That's prancing in the yard.
And of the kittens, soft and warm.
I know that it is hard

When you're so very little,
For I was little, too,
Once upon a time,
When you were just brand new.

Now, I'm your big sister,
And I want you to know
I'll help you every way I can
As you begin to grow.

Stop crying now. I'll help you,
And kiss your tears away.
Let's call Mom to dry us off,
So we can go and play.

© 1994 NKC
City Cousin

CITY COUSIN

A woman from the city
Came out to pay her dues.
She'd heard weekends with country folk
Would really make the news.

She dressed down to blue jeans,
Let down her up-swept hair.
Why, she might even condescend
To see the County Fair!

She thought her country relatives
Might really like to know
That she was quite important.
She'd really make a show.

She drove on past the dirt farms,
To a little dusty lane.
And, sure enough, the folks were home,
She had not come in vain.

She stepped out of her Caddy,
In her dainty, high-heeled shoes,
And called to greet her cousins
In their faded work-day blues.

They welcomed her quite warmly.
It seemed to make their day,
That she had used her precious time
To drive on out their way.

They asked her in for supper,
'Though "dinner" was her word.
The luscious food they served her
Was much better than she'd heard!

No tough ox-tail or possum,
But prime rib, buttered stuff!
And chocolate pie with real sweet cream
All whipped up to a fluff!

She'd thought she'd teach them etiquette,
Bring customs from New York.
But they ate like they'd always known
Just how to hold their fork!

Bakery

Buy World Famous
Poodledown's Pies

Poodledown's
Pies

Humble pie
delivered only
on special order

©1994 NKC
City Cousin

They even used their napkins,
Said "Thank you," yes, and "Please."
They even begged your pardon
If they should have to sneeze.

They drove her to high meadows,
Where flowers were in bloom,
Invited her to spend the night
In a lovely, well kept room.

They spoke of sons at college,
And daughters teaching school.
She'd thought of them as retards
Who couldn't read a rule.

She peeked into their office
While they brewed flavored teas,
And saw there, hanging on the wall,
Their names, and Ph. Ds!

And when shared time was over,
Surprisingly, she'd learned
They were intelligent, sincere and kind,
These relatives she'd spurned!

She drove back to the city,
And vowed that she would try
To savor all their graciousness,
And eat some humble pie.!

© 1995
The Milk Goat

THE MILK GOAT

Grandma was allergic
To cow's milk, later days.
So mama bought a milk goat.
That livened up the ways

That we could spend the mornin's,
Or Sunday afternoon.
For if a hole came in the fence,
That goat would find it soon!

She visited the neighbors
Who really didn't care
To see four legs supportin'
A goat with mangy hair.

Especially when she'd eaten
Some buds about to bloom,
Or was dancing in their garden
Quickly makin' room

For them to replant carrots,
Or corn, or English peas.
Even extra friendly folks
Don't care for tricks like these!

Now, we tried hard to watch her
And fetch her back pronto.
But sometimes she escaped us
And down the road would go.

©1994 N.K.C.

We named that goat Talitha,
For she reminded us
Of a grouchy, gray, old lady
Who was just about to cuss!

Sometimes, she saw the clothesline
Was loaded up with duds.
She munched them and she crunched them
Like a donkey eatin' spuds.

She topped all our petunias,
Strung tin cans down the street.
When it came to messin' up,
She simply wasn't beat!

She stuck her head through windows
And chewed the curtains up.
Once, she swiped our grandma's teeth
Left soakin' in a cup!

We knew we couldn't keep her
But didn't have the heart
To take her to the sale yard,
But "good-bye" thoughts did start.

One early Monday mornin'
She crossed the railroad track.
She took a train to Georgia,
And never did come back!

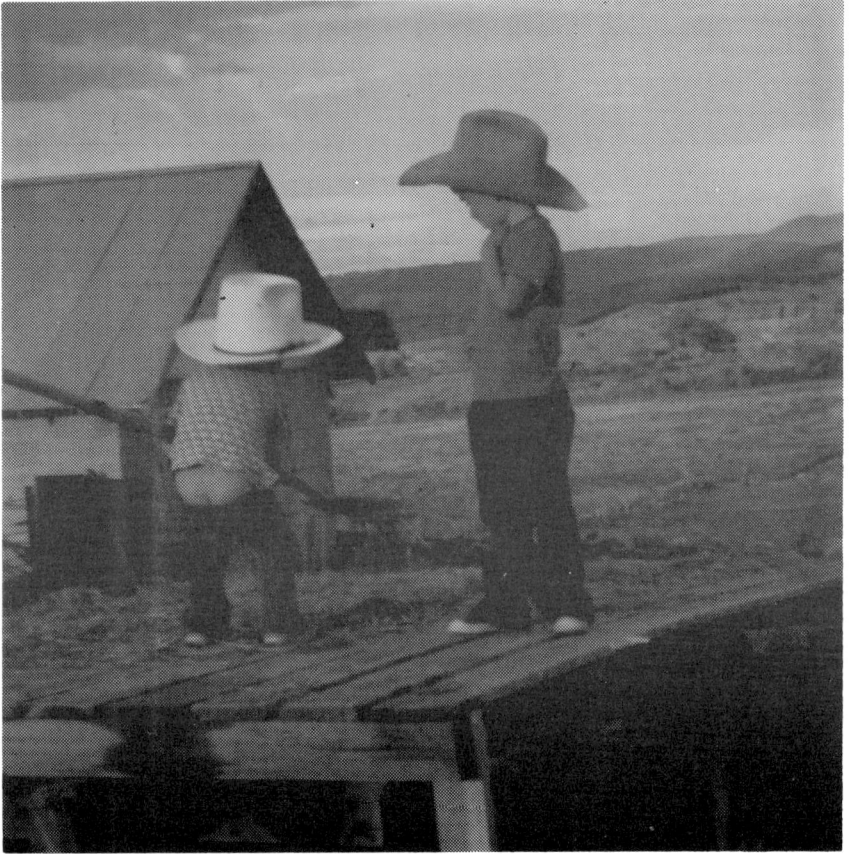

A VISIT AT THE RANCH

"Let's go to Uncle Alfred's
And pitch a little hay.
I know we're not quite big enough,
But maybe we could play

Like I was Dad and you were Unc,
And each one take a hat.
We could pretend that we are big.
What do you think of that?"

"Sounds like fun, but I might need
A push to get clear up.
We'll watch the cows, and maybe see
The kittens and the pup!"

"I heard Aunt Nona has some corn
That grows right on a cob.
And we could check the chicken house
For eggs that we might rob

From fluffy hens that strut around
Out in the chicken yard.
I think we're big enough, don't you?
It shouldn't be too hard."

"Then if we stay for breakfast,
She'd cook the freshest eggs.
I can smell the bacon now.
I need some longer legs!

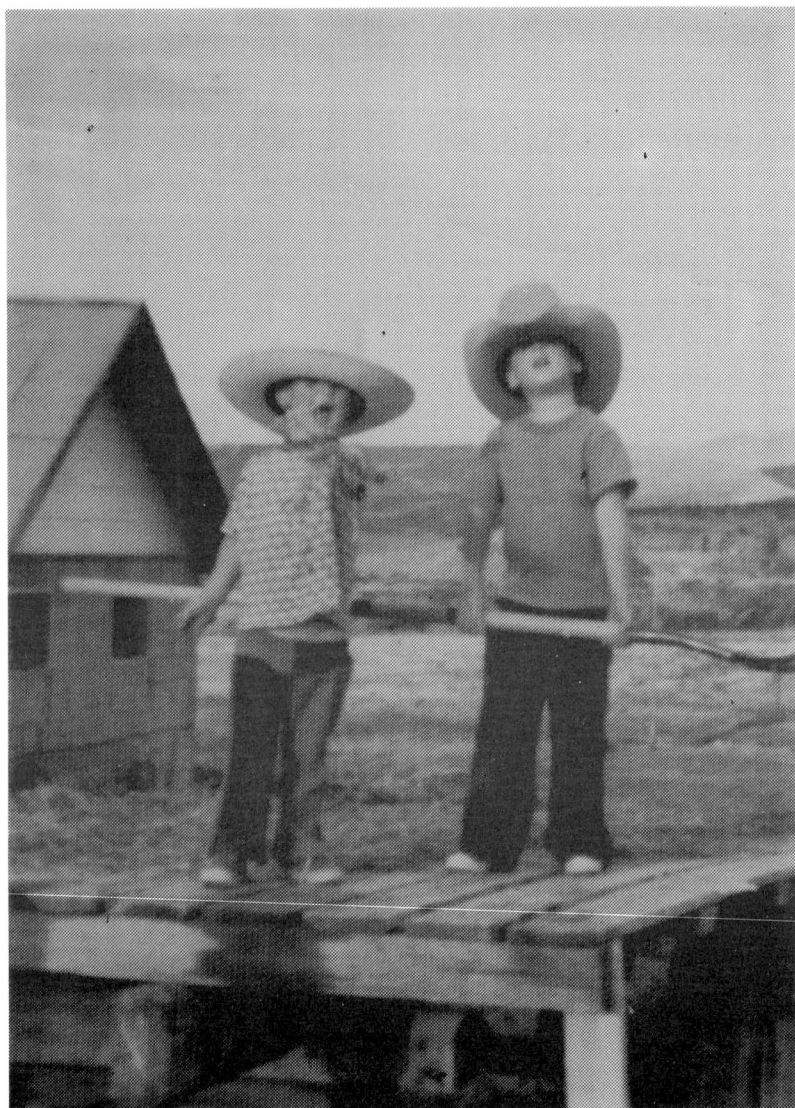

So I could hike up through the grass
That's getting awful tall.
But Dad will take us if we wait.
He thinks we're still too small

To go that far just on our own.
I guess he could be right.
And Mom may come to help us,
And we could stay all night!"

"Maybe if we're good boys
They'll let us pet a calf.
They feel so soft and fuzzy,
And I think almost half

Of them will grow up to be cows,
And others will be steers.
A splinter in your finger?
Don't let Dad see your tears!

He might not think we're big enough
To go and pitch the hay.
I'll dry them quick, so he won't see
Them make you look that way.

All set? I think I hear
Our daddy start the car.
And here comes Mom. It's time to go.
I'm glad it isn't far!"

COWBOYS

When God created cowboys,
He made a different breed.
Some are just plain ornery,
And some help folks in need.

They don't pretend it's easy,
Rising with the sun.
But an extra early start
Helps get all that work done!

They come in every color
Of sunburned shades of red,
A blanket for a bedroll,
The prairie for their bed.

When they're out with the dogies,
The great outdoors their home,
They sing while they are ridin'
Wherever they should roam.

The creek was oft their fountain,
It's water pure and cold.
They might even take some time,
Dismount, and pan for gold.

For wages weren't that much, folks,
For ridin' on the range.
They scarcely paid for boots and hat,
Much less left pocket change!

Once back in the bunkhouse,
They'd change their dusty jeans,
And complement old Charley
For the way he baked the beans.

Tonight there would be bathin'
With water in a tub!
To rid themselves of all that grime,
They'd soak, and then they'd scrub!

They'd use an old tin washboard
To resurrect their socks,
Otherwise, they and their jeans
Would get too stiff for walks.

Sometimes they'd really freshen up
And ride on on to town.
They hoped that they would get a glimpse
Of lass in gingham gown.

A cowboy's life is lonely,
He doesn't ask for much.
He takes his pleasure simple,
No fancy duds and such.

But when they reach the roundup,
Away up in the sky,
They'll march in with the angels,
In that sweet by and by.

BIG SISTER

Why are you the biggest?
Sometimes, I want to be
Big Sister just so you will know
How it feels to be me!

I want to be the first one up
As we start out the day.
And make decisions like you do
Of when and where we'll play.

I think it would be really fun
If I could take a turn.
Just be Big Sister for a day,
Then you would have to learn

About the things I want to do,
But can't because I'm small.
And you could tag along behind
Pretending you were tall!

But since your shoes are much too big,
They might give me a blister.
I guess I'll have to keep my place
And let you be Big Sister.

DAUGHTERS

When God gives us our daughters,
He makes a little plan
To let them bring us happiness
As only daughters can.

He gives them smiles to charm us
In oh, so many ways,
And giggles, hugs and kisses
To brighten up our days.

He lets them understand us,
Respond to young and old,
And share their many secrets
As plans and dreams unfold.

The cares of daily living,
The search for common ground
Just do not seem as pressing,
When daughters are around.

Your life still brings us sunshine,
Gives reason to be glad,
That you, our precious daughter,
Still call us Mom and Dad.

The Shackaroo
©1995 M.N.C.

THE SHUCKAROO

A cowboy and a rancher
Rode out one summer day
To check up on the cattle.
They were not out to play.

They saddled up and started
From the cow camp in the hills.
They dressed to meet the weather
And protect themselves from chills.

Many calves were counted.
They tagged those that were new,
Then tallied up the heifers,
And, of course, the numbers grew.

They peeked into the oakbrush
Where the steers are known to hide,
Looked carefully for cow tracks,
On up the mountain side.

They came upon a critter
Called "Beller" just for short.
She took one wild-eyed look at them
And then began to snort.

Now this cow's disposition
Was the meanest of the lot.
They knew it wasn't sweetened
By the fact she had foot-rot!

©1995 N.K.C.
The Shuckaroo

They'd have to rope and treat her,
And give her shots to boot.
At best, they were good forty miles
From nearest cattle chute

The rancher had the first try.
Ole' Beller slipped his noose
And kicked her heels toward the sky,
Rejoicing she was loose!

She pirouettes and pouts up,
Then charges straight ahead.
They know they best be careful,
Or they could wind up dead!

The cowboy took the next go,
Then looking quite forlorn,
Took note his rope is much too short
And tied to saddle horn...

The noose had settled nicely
Around Ole' Beller's neck
As she was pawing clods of dirt
That beat King Size to heck!

The cow was bawlin', comin',
Arriving much too quick!
The cowboy's thinkin', movin' fast
'Fore he's caught "up the crick!"

He loops around a Quakie,
And he can only hope
It's big enough to hold her
On the short end of the rope!

It flips her like a turnip,
And durn her ornery hide,
She's flailin' air with all four,
As she begins to slide.

The rancher tangled in the rope
And in his chaps and spurs
Was tossed "tail over tincups"
Into the cockleburs.

Old Freckles braced and buckled,
And pulled a shuckaroo.
He left the saddle in the sky,
The startled cowboy too!

The poor old horse was terrified
Of a cow that lacked such grace.
He just stood there tremblin',
With surprise upon his face.

The cowboy and the saddle
Were slidin' in the mud.
The rancher stepped into the scene.
The cow was out for blood!

What happened next you won't believe.
In fact, it's not quite clear.
But Beller's bought her ticket
To the saleyard 'fore next year!

HAPPINESS

Happiness is little girls
That giggle, squeeze, and hug
Each time I lift them from a bath
And stand them on a rug.

Their arms encircle 'round my neck,
And they give kisses rare
As I so gently dry them off
And brush their shining hair.

How could I know the joy they'd bring
Into my lonely life
When I gave up my single ways,
Became a cowboy's wife.

For happiness cannot be bought
Like fancy diamond rings.
It's given to us day by day
In simple, little things,

Like smiles and hugs and
"I love you,"
And oh, so many ways
That lift my heart and bring me joy,
Add sunshine to my days.

Books and Booklets by Nona Kelley Carver

The Tarnish On The Golden Years   Paperback.............12.95
Retirement, an excerpt from The Tarnish
Fully illustrated, 8.5 x 11 inch size.....................................7.00
Middle Age Spread, an excerpt from The Tarnish..........7.00
Bellyache Road, an excerpt from The Tarnish................7.00
Rocking Chair Rhapsodies, from The Tarnish.................7.00
Memories, an excerpt from The Tarnish..........................7.00
Motorcycle Memories
5 x 8.5 Booklet, suitable for mailing................................5.00
Cowboy Poetry-Cowboys, Cookstoves & Catastrophies.......12.95

Mesa County Residents please add 5% sales tax.
Other Colorado Residents please add 3% sales tax.
For all mail orders except Motorcycle Memories, please
add 2.00 postage and handling. Motorcycle booklet, 1.00
postage and handling. Make checks payable to: Carver
Country Poetry, P. O. Box 115 Mesa, CO 81643-0115

Total amount of order...
Amount of tax...
Balance enclosed..

VISA and MASTERCARD orders taken by The Treasure
House Souvenirs and Gifts, Mesa, CO. (970) 268-5642
Hours: 10:00a.m. to 6:00p.m. MST, every day except Tue.
Please allow 6 to 8 weeks for delivery.
A portion of all proceeds will be donated to Plateau
Valley Clinic and Nursing Home, Collbran, Colorado.
Thank you for your order. This page may be copied.